BLACK EYES AND SWEET TALK
A BIBLICAL PERSPECTIVE ON
DOMESTIC VIOLENCE

BY PASTOR MICHAEL NEELY

Copyright © 2018 by Pastor Michael Neely

Disclaimer

This book is intended to provide spiritual guidance and is not intended as a substitute for medical or legal advice. The reader should consult a qualified doctor, lawyer, or counselor as needed in matters relating to his or her specific situation. The author and publisher do not assume, and hereby disclaim, any liability to any party for any loss, damage, or disruption caused by the information provided in this book.

DEDICATION

This book is dedicated to several people who have had a profound influence on my life. First, I dedicate this book to my wife, Tonya Neely, who has been a huge part of my restoration. I have never known a love like ours, and her respect for me drives me to be a better man every day. Throughout the process of writing this book, she constantly encouraged me and never let me forget that my story is important. I thank the Lord every day for the part Tonya has played and continues to play in my emotional and mental restoration.

I also want to dedicate this book to every woman, man, and child who has ever been abused in any shape, form, or fashion. Every survivor of abuse I've counseled over the years is a part of this book. I thought about you while I was writing every chapter. I remember our conversations. I remember your anguished faces. I remember your tears and facial bruises. I remember your struggles with false guilt. I remember seeing the fear on your children's faces. I remember the times you hid behind your sunglasses. I remember when the words to aptly describe your feelings escaped you. I remember the pastor's wives, the doctor's wives, the janitor's wives, and countless others from every walk of life. I remember those of you who struggled with your faith and were told to stay and pray. I also remember the ladies who never came back to see me due to enabling in-laws. This book is for you.

Unfortunately, I also remember the women who died at the hands of their abusers, and that saddens me. One death is too many, and I can only wish that it was only one. This book is for you.

This book is for those who were and still are being set free. This book is for the lady who drove off screaming at the top of her lungs, "I'm Free." This book is for every woman who said, "I'm done and I'm not going back."

Finally, this book is for the abused men who suffer in silence because men are supposed to be strong. I hope reading this book gives you the courage to say, "Me Too."

TABLE OF CONTENTS

Acknowledgments 1

Introduction 3

Chapter One: A Love That Enslaves 5

Chapter Two: When Abnormal Love Becomes Normal Love 9

Chapter Three: Forgiveness And Reconciliation 14

Chapter Four: Why Victims Of Abuse Stay 18

Chapter Five: When To Get Out 22

Chapter Six: How The Church And Clergy Can Help 27

Chapter Seven: I'm Out—Now What? 32

Resources 35

    Family Justice Center Alliance 35

    The Spring of Tampa Bay 35

    Reach Out/Speak Out 35

    New Millennium Community Church 36

    Other Resources 36

About The Author 38

ACKNOWLEDGMENTS

I would like to thank the following people for their contribution, without whom this book would not have been possible.

Kerrick Williams Photography LLC

They set themselves apart by providing passionate and personalized service in every circumstance. Individualized interaction with their clients is a hallmark of their longstanding and flourishing business, bringing a personal approach, attention to detail, and a keen creative eye to every session. I can't thank them enough for all their help in my first endeavor as an author.

Angelique Wynn – Poet, Model, and Makeup Artist Extraordinaire

I've known Angelique for over ten years, and she is one of my spiritual daughters. Her enthusiasm, passion, and dedication to her craft is unparalleled. I'm deeply appreciative of her and the patience it took to make the book cover come to life.

Cynthia Tucker – Editor, Author, and the Founder of Route 66 Ministries

A special thanks to this lady and woman of God. She is a phenomenal editor who walked me through the entire process of developing this book. Every question I asked, she had an answer for or knew where to find it. It was a huge comfort to have someone in my camp who had traveled the book-writing road before.

Natasha Nascimento – Founder and Director of Redefining Refuge

At an unplanned gathering at a Shared Hope conference in Orlando, God used Natasha to encourage me. I and several survivors of trauma were sharing our stories, and after I shared a brief part of my story, God spoke through Natasha. I expressed my hesitancy to put my story in writing, and she said, "God wants you to write the book." It's not as if I had not heard that before, but her tone and countenance resonated with me in a way that made me unable to rest until I wrote the book. Thank you, my friend, for being bold enough to say what the Lord told you to say.

My Book Cover Focus Group

A huge thanks to Katonya Neely, Angelina Adorno, Danielle Sandy, Nicole Hart, Armetha Succeur, Christopher Williams, Mechelle Williams, Barbara Thomas, Jantel Thomas, and Stephanie Neely; your creative input is greatly appreciated.

INTRODUCTION

My exposure to domestic violence started at a very early age. I grew up in a home where the family gathered together every day for breakfast and dinner, with my father at the head of the table. My mother would sit at the other end, and my four brothers, my sister, and I filled in the side chairs.

One particular dinner gathering is forever etched in my psyche. My father's brother, Uncle Walter, was visiting with his girlfriend, Geneva, and we were all having dinner at the kitchen table. Uncle Walter asked Geneva to pass him the ketchup. Unfortunately, the top was loose, so when she passed it to him, the ketchup spilled on his tie. Before she could apologize, my uncle slapped her in the mouth and busted her lip.

My siblings and I sat there in stunned silence as my mother immediately sprang into action. She took Geneva to the bathroom to clean and bandage her wound. My father told his brother to get his belongings and leave the house. After my uncle left, my mother took Geneva home, and we were left behind with my father to deal with the trauma that had just taken place.

We finished dinner, and then my father said something that stayed with me for the rest of my life. He told my three brothers and me to never hit a female no matter what. He told my sister to never let a male hit her. I will never forget the look on his face and the forcefulness of his voice.

That advice has served me well because, later in life, I ended up in an abusive relationship where I could have easily justified using physical retaliation. Between my father's advice and the restraining power of the Holy Spirit, I was victorious. I have never hit a female.

My purpose in writing this book stems from all the bad spiritual advice I received while dealing with my own abusive relationship and the bad advice that continues to be perpetuated from our pulpits and clergy. I'm referring to the typical advice given, as follows:

- Stay and pray.
- The devil is trying to destroy your home, so don't let him.
- God hates divorce (**Malachi 2:16**).

It is my deepest desire and heartfelt prayer that this book will give us a proper biblical perspective on domestic violence and marriage. Until death do us part does not mean until my spouse kills me.

CHAPTER ONE
A LOVE THAT ENSLAVES

The much-anticipated wedding day has arrived. You are walking down the aisle in your perfect dress as your prince charming awaits your arrival at the altar. Your family and friends are all there, and you can feel the love in the air. This is the happiest day of your life. Now it's time to declare your undying love to one another. You both promise to love each other through the good times and the bad times, until death do you part.

The honeymoon is everything you thought it would be, but after returning home and settling in, things begin to change. You do something that irritates your spouse and you're yelled at or even cussed out. This is the first time you have seen this type of behavior, and you are in shock but also in love.

Sometimes being in love causes us to overlook the flaws in our mates. Certainly, a biblical case can be made for doing this. Romans 3:23 says that all have sinned and come short of His glory. Therefore, in marriage, especially when we first fall in love, we overlook all sorts of flaws. However, being in love should not keep us from ignoring serious character flaws like a quick temper, power and control issues, verbal and emotional abuse, bipolar emotions, and how our mates handle stressful situations.

That was my story. I had a storybook wedding on a yacht in Chicago, Illinois in September of 1984. Several of my friends had remarked that it was one of the most beautiful and romantic weddings they had ever witnessed. It was indeed a great day, and my wife and I honeymooned in the Pocono Mountains. Life was good.

Like most married people, we came back from our honeymoon and started living life. I was now a husband and the father of a beautiful three-year-old girl, who I loved as my own and still do. Next to running from God and loving her mother, she was a huge reason I got married. I have always had a soft spot in my heart for children, especially little girls, and she stole my heart.

One thing I learned is that you should never make serious decisions when you are running from God. My beloved mother predicted that my marriage would take a turn for the worse when I became a Christian, but not even she could foresee just how bad it would be. On Saturday, March 30, 1985, at approximately 5:20 p.m., I committed my life to Jesus Christ, and it was the beginning of my mother's prophetic words. My wife at that time had been raised as a Jehovah's Witness, and everyone in her family except her mother was a Jehovah's Witness. When we met back in 1982, she was not practicing her faith, so I really didn't pay much attention to it. However, my mother knew that, eventually, we would clash, and clash we did.

My wife thought I had been led astray by my oldest brother, who was a Christian, and immediately started going back to the Kingdom Hall. She attended church with me one time and never went back. She recommitted herself to the Jehovah's Witnesses and their doctrine and tried in earnest to persuade me that I was wrong. Her intentions were sincere, but you can believe you're right and be sincerely wrong.

It finally dawned on both of us that we were not going to change our religious beliefs, so after months of haggling, we decided to compromise. I would take my daughter to church with me one Sunday and the following Sunday she would go with her mother. Neither of us realized the long-term negative impact this would have on our daughter.

One Sunday morning, we got into a heated argument about who Jesus Christ is. And even though it was my Sunday to take our daughter to church, she wouldn't allow it. Obviously, this was not acceptable to me, so I got dressed and prepared to open the front door to take our daughter to church. My wife stood in front of the door with her hands behind her back and refused to move. I reached for the doorknob and, unbeknownst to me, she had a steak knife in her hand and slashed me across my left wrist.

I stood there in absolute shock and reached for the doorknob again, and she cut me again across the wrist. The blood was flowing, and I retreated to the bathroom to attend to my wounds. It's only by the grace of God that an artery was not cut, which would have put my life in danger. When I came out of the bathroom, she and Monique had gone to the Kingdom Hall. My daughter was four years old, and I wondered how the trauma she had just witnessed affected her. It was then that I realized my mother's prophetic words were coming true.

However, there was hope, and I knew I would find answers at the church I attended. I bandaged my wrist and headed to church. Afterward, I met with some of the elders and told them my story. These elders were wonderful men who loved the Lord and His Word. They also loved me and cared deeply about the sanctity of marriage. However, I now know that they didn't know enough about domestic violence in relation to the Scriptures and gave me the best advice according to the knowledge they had. They said the devil was trying to destroy my marriage (which he was) and that violence was not a biblical reason to leave my marriage. I was so new to Christianity that it never occurred to me to question their advice. The church is not the military, but I was still under authority, which I highly respected, and I yielded to their advice and counsel.

My mind was made up. I was a warrior and no one, including the devil, was going to destroy my marriage. I was going to do whatever it took to win my wife to the Lord. Amazingly, it never occurred to me that I had just been physically abused and that her behavior was a learned behavior. This was simply a spiritual battle and nothing else.

This was the beginning of my journey of denial and blindness to the outbursts of emotional, verbal, and physical abuse headed my way.

My wedding was not a shotgun wedding, and I said those wedding vows of my own free will. The words were ringing in my ears: *What God has joined together, let no man put asunder. I promise to love her until death do us apart.* Love is a very complex emotion sometimes. It can give you so much happiness and so much disappointment. It can make you laugh and make you cry. It can rob you of sound judgment and cause you to end up staying in places no sane person would stay in.

At home that Sunday evening, she did apologize, but her apology didn't match the offense. It's one thing to say *I'm sorry for raising my voice at you* and asking for forgiveness. However, it's a whole other ballgame to apologize for a physical assault and expect immediate forgiveness and reconciliation. The abuser always has a way of making you feel bad for not forgiving them quickly, especially when you are a Christian. Their favorite line is, "You're supposed to forgive me because you're a Christian." Their other favorite line is, "You're not perfect either." I bought it hook, line, and sinker.

The joy that I felt on my wedding day had now been replaced with doubt, fear, false guilt, and an uncertain future, but I was still in love. I had no idea that the same love that has your heart skipping a beat can also enslave and trap you. I now know that a love that abuses the object of that love is not pure love. It may be love, but it's twisted and wounded and should never be tolerated. Love should always set us free and never enslave us.

CHAPTER TWO
WHEN ABNORMAL LOVE
BECOMES NORMAL LOVE

No one gets married to end up divorced. Most people who say "I do" hope that it really is forever. A divorce says that we failed, and no one likes to admit their marriage was a failure, especially if they are Christians. After all, God is love and husbands are commanded to love their wives as Christ loved the church, according to Ephesians 5:25. The Bible teaches us in Romans 5:8 that Christ died for us while we were in our sin. Therefore, we are to love our spouses even when they are not acting lovable.

This is a true statement but, like all biblical truth, it must be examined within the entire context of the Bible. Being a man, I took this mandate very seriously, but I took it further than God intended.

1987 was the year that I came up with what I thought was God's plan. I was employed at *Time Magazine* at the time, and they announced that they were relocating the entire company to Richmond, Virginia and Tampa, Florida. I discussed the issue with my wife, and she thought it would be a great idea to relocate. I was offered a promotion, which meant more money and opportunity for growth within the company. However, my main reason for agreeing to the relocation was for spiritual reasons. I figured it would take the Lord two years to save her, change her, and transform her. We would move back to Chicago and go into ministry and all would be well. Obviously, I was wrong. I am convinced that the Lord wanted me to relocate, but the two-year plan was my idea. Proverbs 16:9 says, "In their hearts humans plan their course, but the Lord establishes their steps."

My plan backfired. Instead of her Jehovah's Witness faith getting weaker, it got stronger, which meant more arguments and angry moments. Love is a strange emotion, and if it's not properly understood, it can do more damage than good. There were what I call honeymoon periods. The marriage was good. We got along and laughed a lot, and those were the times where I figured I could love her into the kingdom. However, there was always a fear of what was bubbling beneath the surface. I now realize that the arguments ceased only when we didn't discuss our religious differences. Peace at all costs is not peace. It's a false peace that will eventually explode at any given moment. I am not condoning constant and habitual disagreement, but couples need to have the difficult conversations if their relationship is to be one of quality.

We all tend to see just one side of anything, especially when it comes to Scripture. Love is viewed most of the time from a romanticized viewpoint. Love as a word describes an emotion with vastly differing degrees of intensity. We can say we love ice cream and chocolate, and we can pledge our love to a husband or wife until our dying breath.

Love is one of the most powerful emotions we can experience. Humans crave love from the moment of existence, and the Bible tells us that God is love. For Christian believers, love is the true test of genuine faith. Four unique forms of love are found in the Bible. They are communicated through four Greek words: Eros, Storge, Philia, and Agape.

For the purpose of this book, I want to focus on just two: Agape and Eros. Agape **(Pronounced: Uh-GAH-pay)** is the highest of the four types of love in the Bible. This term defines God's immeasurable, incomparable love for humankind. It is the divine love that comes from God. Agape love is perfect, unconditional, sacrificial, and pure. Jesus Christ demonstrated this kind of divine love to his Father and to all humanity in the way he lived and died. Eros (**Pronounced: AIR-ohs**) is the Greek word for sensual or romantic love. The term originated from the mythological Greek goddess of love, sexual desire, physical attraction, and physical love. Even though the term is not found in the Old Testament, the biblical book Song of Solomon vividly portrays the passion of erotic love.

I am convinced that Eros love combined with a misunderstanding of Agape love causes some spouses to stay in domestic violence relationships. One example is that our physical attraction to a person can blind us to seeing their severe character flaws, especially their power and control issues. The courtship is wonderful. The person wants to be with us all the time because they love us so much. The Eros attraction is so strong that we can't see their behavior as abnormal—after all, it's love. Soon thereafter, we become isolated from our friends and family because we are so in love. The abuser has now gained control of our time and, most of all, our mindset.

Pure biblical Agape love desires the best for the object of that love. Jesus Christ died for us because He wanted the absolute best for us. He left the glory of heaven, became a man, died on the cross, and rose from the dead. He did this so that all of us would have the chance to gain eternal life and salvation. His pursuit was relentless, and no stone was left unturned. However, the one thing He never did in His pursuit of us was to sin.

All abuse is sin, especially physical, emotional, financial, and verbal abuse. The question is what should love look like in this environment? I stated earlier that Agape love wants what's best for the object of its love. This is the side of love that we don't fully think through. When we allow another person to abuse us in any form, we become a willing participant in their sin. They are sinning against God, themselves, and the person who is being abused. The abuser is engaged in the desecration of a person created in God's image, and if we allow it, then so are we. The irony is that the abuser is also created in God's image; therefore, the desecration is doubled. If there is any chance for the abuser to change, there must be severe consequences motivated by Agape love. I walked out of my own situation because I was tired, depressed, and wanted peace at all costs. I now realize that it wasn't just for my own good but for hers also.

Finally, we teach best by what we do rather than what we say. Every parent wants to teach their children what healthy biblical love looks like. Those days of "do as I say and not what I do" were never effective to begin with.

When we stay in an abusive relationship or marriage, we are teaching our children that this is what love looks like. They are being taught that love means verbal, emotional, mental, and physical abuse. Boys are taught that it's okay to hit girls when you're irritated or when you can't have your way. Girls are taught that when a boy hits you, it's because he loves you. If the abuser is a woman, then the effect is just the opposite.

The longer you stay in an abusive relationship, the longer it becomes normal. It's like something that kidnapping victims and captives go through. Stockholm syndrome, or capture-bonding, is a psychological phenomenon described in 1973 in which hostages express empathy and sympathy and have positive feelings toward their captors, sometimes to the point of defending and identifying with them. This can happen in abusive relationships, especially because of the love factor.

I will never forget when I was counseling a 19-year-old girl whose boyfriend had given her a black eye. I was livid until I found out that she hit him first. I still don't believe the man should have hit her back and as hard as he did, but self-defense reflexes kick in automatically sometimes. When I asked why she felt it was okay to hit him, she stated that her mother hit her father off and on throughout their marriage. In other words, that was her normal.

That's when it dawned on me that by staying in my own abusive situation so long, I had allowed the abnormal to become my normal.

My mind was besieged by the thought of what I had taught my own daughter by staying so long. This is one way generational curses are passed on. It is essential that we think through what kind of example we are setting for our children and our grandchildren. A normal relationship is giving—not self-serving, not abusive, and not controlling. An abnormal relationship is the exact opposite.

The most important thing a parent can do for their child is to make sure they don't spend their adulthood overcoming their childhood. Therefore, we must never allow the abnormal to become the norm. The well-being of our children and grandchildren could very well depend on it.

Chapter Three
Forgiveness And
Reconciliation

The typical cycle of an abusive relationship is one of habitual forgiveness and reconciliation. The abuser offends and then expects immediate forgiveness regardless of the depth of the offense. Unfortunately, most churches teach that forgiveness and reconciliation are one and the same. Therefore, not only are we biblically bound to forgive but also to reconcile. A person with strong faith based upon a weak theology is a danger to themselves as well as others. Lumping forgiveness and reconciliation together as a biblical mandate has done a ton of damage to abused women. The very faith that is supposed to set people free keeps the abused in prison.

Forgiveness is a dominant theme throughout the Bible. The act of forgiving does not come easy for most of us. Our instinct is to recoil in self-protection when we've been injured. We don't naturally overflow with mercy, grace, and understanding when we've been wronged. Forgiveness is a choice we make. It is a decision of our will, motivated by obedience to God and his command to forgive. The Bible instructs us to forgive as the Lord forgave us: "Bear with each other and forgive one another if any of you has a grievance against someone. Forgive as the Lord forgave you" (Colossians 3:13).

Lewis B. Smedes wrote in his book, *Forgive and Forget*, "When you release the wrongdoer from the wrong, you cut a malignant tumor out of your inner life. You set a prisoner free, but you discover that the real prisoner was yourself." Therefore, it is essential that we forgive those who abuse us because it empties them of their power. But the mandate to forgive does not always mean reconciling with the offender. Let's talk about reconciliation.

Reconciliation comes from the Greek family of words that has its roots in *allasso (ajllavssw)*. The meaning common to this word group is "change" or "exchange." Reconciliation involves a change in the relationship between God and man or man and man. It assumes there has been a breakdown in the relationship, but now there has been a change from a state of enmity and fragmentation to one of harmony and fellowship. In Romans 5:6–11, Paul says that before reconciliation we were powerless, ungodly, sinners, and enemies; we were under God's wrath (v. 9). Because of change or reconciliation, we become new creatures. "Therefore, if anyone is in Christ, he is a new creation; the old has passed away; behold, the new has come!" (2 Cor. 5:17 ESV).

Reconciliation has to do with the relationships between God and man or man and man. God reconciles the world to himself (2 Cor 5:18). Reconciliation takes place through the cross of Christ or the death of Christ. Second Corinthians 5:18 says that God reconciled us to himself through Christ. God reconciles us to himself through the death of his Son (Rom. 5:1).

The Bible commands us to always forgive people their wrongs against us no matter how great the offense. We have always sinned against God more than others have sinned against us, and since God offers his forgiveness regardless of our offenses, he expects us to do the same (Matt. 18:21–35).

You can forgive people who have hurt you deeply, but it is not always possible or right to reconcile with abusive, hurtful, or unrepentant people. The Bible says forgiveness is a choice one individual can make without the consent of another. The Bible also says, however, that reconciliation needs two parties to agree regarding the restoration of the relationship. You can have forgiveness without reconciliation. However, you cannot have reconciliation without forgiveness.

There are three types of reconciliation. You can have full reconciliation, partial reconciliation, or no reconciliation at all. The common denominator is always full forgiveness. The variable is to what level reconciliation is glorifying to God and safe for those involved. God always calls every Christian to forgive others, but God does not call us to always be reconciled. Forgiveness can be done in your heart between you and God. Reconciliation must involve the willful choice of two people or parties. In the case of abuse, it is not always wise to automatically reconcile.

Additionally, it is against Scripture to reconcile with people who claim to be Christians and yet refuse to repent, by their actions, of the sins you have pointed out to them (Matthew 18:17, 1 Corinthians 5:12–13). When people are retaliatory, threatening, a risk to you, a risk to others, or consistently living contrary to the Scriptures, it is your biblical obligation to forgive but not reconcile. Remember, love wants what is ultimately best for the object of that love. There are consequences to abusive behavior, and sometimes it means loving that person from a distance. You can and must forgive them, but reconciliation is not a mandate. I use the 80/20 rule, which I received from Dr. Charles Stanley. If there is a 20 percent chance the offense will be repeated, there will be no reconciliation. The offender will be loved from a distance.

The first act of domestic violence recorded in Scripture is found in Genesis 4 when Cain murders his brother Abel. The Lord calls Cain on the carpet about his sinful act toward his brother. I think we can deduce from the text that at some point, he had a conversation with his parents, Adam and Eve. I'm sure they forgave him, but God issued a severe penalty for his sinful act. In Genesis 4:12–16, God informs Cain that when he works the land, it will no longer yield any crops to him. He also told Cain that he would become a restless wanderer across the earth. The Bible says he left the presence of the Lord.

He was still his parents' son, but he probably never saw them again. There was forgiveness, but the nature of his relationship with his parents was changed by the geographical consequences of his sin.

The basic rule of thumb when it comes to reconciliation is to do what will bring the most glory to God while also promoting the most healing for the human hearts involved. Instead of forgiving, staying, and praying, it is sometimes wise to forgive, leave, and pray.

CHAPTER FOUR
WHY VICTIMS OF ABUSE STAY

I t's very easy to Monday morning quarterback after the game has been played on Sunday afternoon. You review the plays that were called or were not called. You question the coach's decisions at critical moments and wonder why a different decision was not made. We all tend to do this, especially as it relates to relationships.

Admittedly, I too have wondered from time to time why I stayed so long in an abusive relationship. I think all of us have some regrets about past decisions made, but regret is a worthless emotion. Living in regret is dangerous because there is nothing you can do about the past. Therefore, I choose to live in my present and make better decisions for my future. However, all of us should learn from our past and gain more wisdom.

One reason I stayed is because of my biblical convictions. My blind devotion to *no divorce at any cost* was the driving force behind my staying in an unhealthy marriage. I am a firm believer in the sanctity of marriage. There is no doubt in my mind that a two-parent (a father and a mother) household is the best environment to raise a child in. I also believe that an abusive home brings no glory to God and is detrimental to the emotional, mental, spiritual, and physical well-being of all involved.

In 2000, Paige Patterson was asked about women who are abused by their husbands. Here's what the former president of Southwestern Baptist Theological Seminary said:

> It depends on the level of abuse to some degree. I
> have never in my ministry counseled that anybody

seek a divorce, and I do think that's always wrong counsel. There have been, however, an occasion or two when the level of the abuse was serious enough, dangerous enough, immoral enough that I have counseled temporary separation and the seeking of help. I would urge you to understand that that should happen only in the most serious of cases.... More often, when you face abuse, it is of a less serious variety.[1]

Patterson's statement seems to suggest that divorce due to abuse is not biblically sanctioned. In my opinion, that understanding isn't really a biblical one. Many Christians, especially clergy, fear sanctioning divorce after abuse because it's not explicitly mentioned as a cause to end a marriage, even though the Bible speaks frankly about violence and abuse.

In Psalm 11:5, the psalmist, referring to God, says he hates the one who does violence and abuses. There are more passages that say that God hates the violent and the oppressor. One thing I have learned from my own experiences is that we must think through our doctrinal positions. What are the logical conclusions of what we say we believe?

It's essential because too often in the past, religious traditions have been used to defend an abusive patriarchy, to bind victims to marriage commitments that are undermined by intimate violence, to encourage people to "offer up" suffering rather than change the conditions that cause it.

---

[1] "What the Bible Says about Abuse Within Marriage," *Christianity Today* (May 2018): accessed October 16, 2018, https://www.christianitytoday.com/ct/2018/may-web-only/domestic-violence-bible-divorce-abuse.html.

It's essential because speaking out about domestic violence as a violation of God's love can give victims strength to seek a better way. It's essential because naming domestic violence as evil can help call perpetrators to account — and perhaps to repentance and treatment.

When Christians talk about the ideals of marriage, particularly when discussing Ephesians 5, we need to be sure that we can account for the reality of marriage. For many, far from being the context of mutuality and partnership, intimate relationships can be the most precarious and dangerous context for women. Indeed, perpetrators of violence and abuse are most typically those who are well-known, often romantic partners or spouses, rather than strangers.

When preachers emphasize verse 21 — "Submit to one another out of reverence for Christ" — they make clear the importance of challenging the gender hierarchy that justifies violence. Yet here, even at its best, preaching on this text may inadvertently communicate a message that seems to implicitly endorse abusive patterns.

Yet, for women for whom this equality is not taken for granted, at least in practice, being told to submit to another can have the negative consequence of reinforcing a culturally conditioned inequality.

Rather than recognizing an abusive imbalance of power or abusive speech and actions, she may be encouraged to deny her own needs — even at the risk of her health. She may see aggression and turmoil as typical parts of a good Christian marriage that can be overcome. If she simply negates her own needs for those of her partner and marriage, everyone will be happy.

Another reason people stay in an abusive relationship is fear of reprisal by the abuser. This is especially true for women. The decision to leave an intimate partner escalates the risk of violence. For women who are being abused, this significantly increases the likelihood of her death at his hands, with the danger ratcheting up for pregnant women. Too many cannot go back home and have nowhere else to go; therefore, they are more vulnerable to their abusers.

Intimate partner violence is a pervasive problem in our society. Moreover, while intimate partner violence affects men in addition to women, it disproportionally victimizes women. According to the Centers for Disease Control and Prevention, as many as 47.1 percent of women experience at least one act of psychological aggression in their lifetime. This aggression can turn physically violent: 31.5 percent of women experience physical violence in their lifetime, while 22.3 percent of women are victimized at least once by a severe act of violence. Intimate partners also perpetrate sexual violence. About 8.8 percent of women are raped and another 15.8 percent are sexually victimized by a partner in their lifetime. Finally, 9.2 percent of women are stalked by a partner to the point of fearing for their physical safety.

Lack of financial resources is another reason victims of abuse stay instead of leaving. Many women are very dependent on the monetary resources of their husband, and that doubles if children are involved. Their reality says, "Where will I go? How will the kids and I eat? How can I afford to put a roof over our heads?" It's also unfortunate that domestic violence shelters get the bad reputation of being places nobody should live in.

Enabling in-laws is another reason victims of abuse stay. Many times, the abuser grew up in an abusive home where his father was an abuser and his mother stayed. Therefore, when the abuser's parents find out that he is abusing his wife, they counsel her to stay. They counsel her to drop the restraining order if she filed one against him. If the abuser is arrested for hitting her, she is blamed for his arrest. The pressure, along with the false guilt she has suffered from the abuser, can be daunting.

As discussed previously, improperly understanding forgiveness, reconciliation, and love are all reasons victims stay. I hope this chapter helps those of you who have loved ones or friends involved in abusive relationships to have more compassion and understanding.

CHAPTER FIVE
WHEN TO GET OUT

I'm sure we've all heard the phrase, "sick and tired of being tired." The statement indicates that when a person is tired enough of being tired, they will do something to change their situation. I would agree that it's true in most situations but not in a lot of domestic violence relationships. Depending on the type of abuse, the longevity of the relationship, who the abuser is, religious beliefs about abuse, and other factors, being sick and tired is not enough.

There must be a fundamental shift in a person's mindset that finally decides, "I don't deserve to be abused, and I want a better life." For those who have strong biblical convictions, there must be a shift in how they view God and what He expects from us. Is God tyrannical or loving? Is He happy that I'm staying in an abusive relationship or is He happy that I'm finally leaving? One question to ask yourself if you are in an abusive relationship is, "What's the price tag of being mentally, emotionally, and spiritually healthy?" I have personally concluded that peace of mind is the most valuable commodity a person can have. It is priceless.

The day I decided to leave was not the day I left. There are so many factors involved in leaving, and a safety plan is crucial. However, you can make up your mind that you are leaving and begin to make plans as soon as you can. The day I decided to leave was like any other day, except my ex and I got into an argument about who Jesus is. I now look back and realize that most of our arguments were over the Bible and whether Jesus Christ is God or not. However, people with abusive tendencies have all sorts of triggers. Unfortunately, Jesus was her trigger.

I sensed the discussion had taken a turn for the worse and I backed off. Unfortunately, her anger was unleashed in such a way that, had it not been for God's grace, I probably would have been dead. A very sharp object was thrown at the back of my head; it barely missed me and embedded itself in the kitchen wall. I remember vividly the look on her face when she realized what had almost happened. She hated what she had done and, like many people trapped in ugly behavior, she was remorseful.

But I have learned that real repentance takes place when steps are taken to correct or cure the behavior. In many cases, for your own sanity, you must let the abuser change for someone else if they decide to change at all.

I remember saying to myself at that moment that I was done. I never said it to her, but my mind was made up. I checked out emotionally and mentally. I didn't leave for another couple of years physically, but mentally, I was already gone. In every abusive relationship, there are what I call honeymoon periods. Those are the times when there is no emotional or physical abuse. I experienced many of those times, and sometimes the good times can cloud your judgment about the bad times. That's why I advise people to leave as soon as possible, but leave safely and not haphazardly.

The first time a person puts a hand on you is one time too many. The abuser should be called on the carpet immediately, and you should leave the home or ask the abuser to leave, if possible. Any hope of saving the marriage or relationship hinges on being ruthless in your stance that abuse is totally unacceptable behavior. The abuser must seek immediate help, and you must have full access to the counselor, psychiatrist, or doctor during the help period. Guidelines for restoring trust and guidelines for accountability must be put in place. In my 12 years of domestic violence counseling, I have yet to meet an abuser who has changed while he or she was with the same person they abused.

My final illumination came when I was so depressed that I needed to get away and clear my mind. I flew up to Chicago to visit my brother for a week. I was in full-time ministry at First Baptist Church of College Hill, which I loved and believed God had called me to. Yet I was silently living in an emotionally unhealthy state. I always had a third-degree deodorant approach to life. You never let people see you sweat. A leader is never vulnerable. I always had my game face on in public. However, underneath my game face, I was depressed, discouraged, and insecure about who I was.

One morning after being in Chicago for three or four days, I woke up with this incredible and indescribable feeling of euphoria. I was so full of energy and pep that I went running. It was mind-blowing, and I didn't know what was happening to me. Afterward, I returned to my brother's house and sat on the front porch.

My brother came out and joined me and asked how I was feeling. I replied that I didn't know how to explain because these feelings were so new to me. I'll never forget how he looked at me and the words that came out his mouth. He said, "Michael, for the first time in a long time, you are experiencing a taste of what it feels like to be emotionally and mentally healthy." I realized then that I had been trapped in an abnormal relationship so long that I had forgotten what normal felt like. My abnormal had become my normal in more ways than one. God met me on that front porch, and I knew I could not go back and live in abnormality any longer. I was done.

I flew back to Tampa and within 30 days, I moved out. I wanted peace of mind so badly that I gave my ex everything, including the house. I moved into an 8 by 18 room in Ybor City, and as it turned out, my landlord was a Jehovah's Witness. I guess God does have a sense of humor after all. I would love to say that life after that was all peaches and cream, but it wasn't. My money was funny, and my change was strange. Life was in many ways more difficult than it had been before I left. Leaving was supposed to rectify everything and give me peace, but I learned you don't recover from 15 years of abnormality overnight.

Divorce is like a death, and it doesn't matter who or what caused the divorce. No one can adequately prepare you for the wave of emotions you will experience. The feelings of failure are overwhelming. Most people don't get married to end up divorced. The number of negative responses I received from brothers and sisters in Christ was amazing.

It all came crashing down on me one lonely Friday night as I lay restlessly in my twin bed staring at my four-foot refrigerator. This was not my idea of walking in my purpose and fulfilling my God-given destiny. I cried out to God and He met me at my point of need that night. He reminded me that having a future of quality would cost me something. I picked up my Bible and turned to Joel 2:25–27, which says,

> I will repay you for the years the locusts have eaten—the great locust and the young locust, the other locusts and the locust swarm—my great army that I sent among you. You will have plenty to eat, until you are full, and you will praise the name of the Lord your God, who has worked wonders for you; never again will my people be shamed. Then you will know that I am in Israel, that I am the Lord your God, and that there is no other; never again will my people be shamed.

I realize that a correct exegesis of this passage emphasizes Israel and their disobedience and subsequent return to the Lord. God sent the locusts to humble them. However, I claimed this passage for myself because abuse has a way of eating at your emotional, mental, and spiritual health and devouring your peace of mind. I'm aware that God will not put any of us in a time machine and give us a do-over, but the promise in this passage for me was as follows: "Walk with me through this process and trust me. I will make your future of such quality that your past will pale in comparison and peace of mind will be your future companion." He has done that and more.

I have no regrets about leaving. My biggest struggle for years was fighting my regret for not leaving sooner. Peace of mind is priceless. Emotional, mental, and spiritual health are priceless. This is a gift we all deserve, and it's worth fighting for.

CHAPTER SIX
HOW THE CHURCH AND CLERGY CAN HELP

In the past, the church has adopted the stay-and-pray approach. This approach is borne out of a systematic theology rooted in Malachi 2:16, which states that God hates divorce. Therefore, divorce must be avoided at all costs, regardless of the consequences of staying in an abusive relationship.

Unfortunately, this approach has subjected many women and men (mostly women) to unnecessary humiliation, verbal and emotional abuse, physical abuse, and on too many occasions, death. It wasn't until I left my own abusive marriage that I discovered how deeply entrenched the stay-and-pray mentality was in the church.

I was conducting a Bible study one Wednesday evening in 2001 at First Baptist Church of College Hill about marriage and divorce. It was like any other Bible study until a lady raised her hand and asked, "What does the Bible have to say about domestic violence in relation to marriage and divorce?" Suddenly, almost every person in attendance leaned forward. There was a spirit of anticipation and anxiety permeating the entire sanctuary. Every facial expression in the place seemed to be asking the same question that had been asked verbally. Admittedly, I hesitated because I knew the difficulty of the question and the prevalent old-school mentality.

I remember carefully walking through such passages as Malachi 2, Matthew 5:31–32, Mark 10:2–12, 1 Corinthians 7:11–13, 1 Corinthians 7:39, and other passages. For instance, 1 Corinthians 7:11–13 deals with a marriage between an unbeliever and a believer. Only God can discern the intents of a person's heart, but we can judge actions. In my experience, most abusers who go to church are wolves masquerading as sheep. The church needs to have the courage to pronounce such men as spiritually dead based on Romans 7:1–4. My final statement was that God rejoices when any of His children are no longer under bondage to abuse and that domestic violence breaks the marital covenant. I knew my response was radical to some, life-giving to some, and blatantly heretical to others.

It was not until the next day that I fully realized the impact of that Bible study. There were approximately 100 people in attendance that Wednesday evening, and the next day my phone was ringing off the hook. I must have fielded about 15 phone calls from women who had been there.

I was stunned to find out that all of them were being abused in some way. The real shocker was that some of them were in attendance with the man who was abusing them. One lady's story stood out more than the rest. I will call her Sarah to protect her identity. She informed me that her husband had torn up my Bible study handout and told her to dismiss everything she heard that evening. He dropped her off at home while he left to go get high on drugs. When he came back home, he physically and sexually abused her. Suffice it to say the details were horrific and bone-chilling.

My first question was, "How long has this been going on?" She said, "For almost 17 years." Then she said, "You are the first pastor I have ever heard say that it was ok to leave." She had been a member of several prominent churches in the Tampa Bay area, and the advice was the same every time: "You should stay and pray." When you tell a person that, you are implying that the abuse is in some way partially their fault. It sends the message that she should have more faith that God will fix him, or she isn't praying hard enough. It sends the message that any man is better than no man.

My heart was broken over her suffering all those years because she thought God would be angry if she left. However, I could relate because there were times when I felt the same way. I told her that if she ever desired to leave, I would help her. Later that same day, she called and took me up on my offer. She had arranged for her family and friends to help her leave while her husband was at work. I showed up the next day in my work clothes prepared to do a lot of heavy lifting.

Unbeknownst to me, that was not her plan. She didn't want help physically but spiritually. She asked me to go to my car and bring back my Bible. I did so and asked what she wanted me to do next. This was her story and her life; therefore, she should set the agenda. She reminded me of the story of Moses when he held up his arms at the Red Sea and God's people were delivered from the hand of Pharaoh. She said, "Until the cars and trucks are packed, I would like you to stand here on the front porch and hold the Bible up like Moses raised his staff." I complied and stood there for approximately an hour switching arms while holding the Bible up like a staff to heaven. It was a defining moment for me. God's Word was being used to set a captive free!

Finally, the cars and trucks were packed, and we were all about to drive off when, suddenly, I heard Sarah call my name. She got out of her car and I got out of mine. Sarah stood in front of me with tears running down her face and said, "Pastor, tell me one more time that God wants me free and that He is happy that I'm finally leaving."

With tears in my own eyes, I said, "God wants you free, and He is smiling right now."

She hugged me and thanked me and got back in her car. The window was rolled down, and I heard her shouting, "I'm free, I'm free" as the driver drove off. I never saw her again, and I hope she is still free and telling her story to help others who are trapped in abusive marriages and relationships. That was the day I decided I would try to help anyone who would listen understand that abuse is not God's purpose or design for their life.

The church should reflect Jesus Christ in terms of setting people free and not keeping them trapped. The faith that is supposed to liberate us should never be used to enslave us. I'm a strong believer in the sanctity of marriage but an even stronger believer in the sanctity of life. *Till death do us part* doesn't mean *until my spouse kills me.*

The church needs to rethink its position on domestic violence and marriage. Unfortunately, most seminaries and Bible colleges only give domestic violence lip service and haven't developed a sound theological position on the issue.

It should be a requirement for all clergy to understand the nuts and bolts of domestic violence and the dos and don'ts. For instance, one of the biggest mistakes pastors make is trying to counsel the abuser and the victim of abuse together. The victim should be counseled alone so the counselor can get the truth about how bad the abuse is. The victim will never tell the whole truth in front of the abuser for fear of reprisal.

Physical abuse is a crime. If someone on the street hits us, we would call the police. For some reason, we refrain from doing so in intimate relationships. Churches should have the courage to report physical abuse and encourage others to do the same.

Churches should make it clear from their pulpits that intimate partner abuse will not be tolerated on any level. Clergy need a paradigm shift when they preach on marriage from Ephesians chapter 5. Arguably the most frequently quoted verses in the entire Christian Scripture to support male dominance and encourage female subservience, Ephesians 5:21–33 has been misused for centuries. While this practice in and of itself may not cause domestic violence, it offers men a pathway to commit horrific acts against women (and children) without fear of accountability.

Because women hardly had any rights in the days of biblical antiquity, it seems to me that the emphasis in Ephesians 5 is on the husband and not the wife. Paul puts most of the emphasis on a man loving his wife as Christ loved the church. A wife should never follow her husband into sin, and abuse of any sort is sin. Most sermons emphasize the wife submitting to her husband, and abusers love those sermons. Unwittingly, many clergymen have helped abusers by not qualifying the text and explaining that submission is mutual in a marriage, according to Ephesians 5:21. The rest of the text explains what that looks like. Most women cringe today when they hear the word submission because it has been taught incorrectly.

Another way churches can help is by developing relationships with the domestic violence organizations in their cities and communities. I have had the privilege of serving as an executive board member and chaplain of the now defunct Family Justice Center. It is one of the finest organizations I've ever had the privilege of being a part of. It was a one-stop shop for victims of domestic violence. The Spring of Tampa Bay is another fine organization that I am proud to be affiliated with. They have been at the forefront of domestic violence since 1977. These organizations need volunteers as well as financial support to continue to serve victims of domestic violence.

I would also encourage churches to develop domestic violence support groups in their churches. Victims of domestic violence need all the love and support they can get, especially from the faith community. Finally, every church, regardless of their denominational affiliation, should stand in solidarity and declare unequivocally that nobody deserves to be abused. Nobody means absolutely nobody.

CHAPTER SEVEN
I'M OUT—NOW WHAT?

The aftermath of coming out of an abusive relationship can be unnerving. Your first feeling may be relief, but it may soon be replaced by doubt. Emotionally healthy thinking doesn't happen overnight. The road to being emotionally, mentally, and spiritually healthy takes time. Thoughts of failure, wondering, *Did I make the right decision*, and the negative voices of the critics can be overwhelming. If there are children involved, they may be acting out because of what they are feeling and experiencing.

Even after victims are physically safe and bodily wounds have healed, emotional and psychological scars run deep. Domestic violence can have severe spiritual implications as well. Victims may distrust God. Why would He allow such a thing to happen? Is He trustworthy? Does He really love me? Where was He when I was being abused? Walking through the healing process takes time. The emotional reaction to the situation must come. It is appropriate to express anger over the abuse. If we do not acknowledge the severity of the situation—the anger, the confusion, the hurt, the shame, etc.—we cannot heal from it. Too often, victims are prematurely hurried into forgiveness. Ultimately, forgiveness is what will set a victim free, but true forgiveness cannot be extended if the scars of the abuse are not first acknowledged and dealt with.

Intellectually, you know you made the right decision, but old habits of thinking die hard. I remember experiencing many feelings of inadequacy because I certainly was not perfect. I made mistakes like we all do, and you ask yourself, *what could I have done better?* There's nothing wrong with being introspective and trying to become a better person. However, I had to keep reminding myself that I was fearfully and wonderfully made. Therefore, regardless of my imperfections, I deserved better.

Depending on the length of the relationship and the lethality of the abuse, the loneliness can lead you down another bad road. The worst thing you can do is enter another relationship too soon.

The feelings of loneliness and the God-given need to be loved, cherished, and respected can cause us to end up in the arms of the same abuser again. Even if we don't return to the original abuser, we may end up with another abuser. This happens because victims of abuse don't take time to heal. Because I was a preacher, I felt like I didn't need any counseling. I had checked out of the marriage emotionally for years before the final divorce. I kept telling myself that there was nothing wrong with me. I think part of that was because of my male ego. We men do struggle with being vulnerable and transparent.

I remember trying to date a young lady who I thought was perfect. After I told her my story of abuse, she had enough sense not to date me. I was very frustrated because I kept telling myself there was nothing wrong with me.

One day I learned that I was wrong and she was right. It was my birthday and she and her best friend took me to lunch. After lunch, the three of us were sitting in my car and she handed me a gift bag with three figurines inside: a preacher, a church, and a choir. She then said, "That's you and your choir that God is going to give you."

Then it happened. I was so overwhelmed with this small token of affirmation that I started sobbing uncontrollably. I could not believe what was happening to me. I knew then that I needed help. It was delusional for me to think I was not affected by the abnormality of my previous marriage. Soon thereafter, I sought professional help, and it was one of the best decisions I've ever made concerning my emotional health.

Many abusive men are still predators on the prowl. When you tell them your story, these men spot your weakness and before you know it, you're back where you started. Be careful who you tell your story to. Everyone doesn't have your best interest at heart.

All victims of abuse need aftercare, which may look different for each person. However, I am convinced that professional counseling, trauma counseling, domestic violence support groups, and being able to tell your story in a non-judgmental setting go a long way in helping victims become healthy.

Also, victims should be careful which organizations they seek help from and become affiliated with. Some organizations will exploit your story for their financial gain. One example is coercing you to tell your story before you are ready to do so. Another example is controlling your decisions about your future instead of allowing you to make decisions for yourself. Healthy domestic violence organizations seek to empower the victim instead of controlling them. You can easily become a victim of organizational abuse. As I mentioned, The Spring of Tampa Bay is a great organization to seek help from. Reach Out and Speak Out is another organization in the Bay area that is a great advocate for victims of domestic violence.

Finally, for those who are in churches where the stay-and-pray mentality still exists, I encourage you to talk to your leaders. Hopefully, they are willing to listen and learn about how to handle domestic violence in their churches in a way that always puts safety first. However, if they are not willing to change, then I encourage you to leave and find a church that promotes the sanctity of life over the sanctity of marriage. Remember, *till death do us part* does not mean *until my spouse kills me.*

RESOURCES

Family Justice Center Alliance

The Family Justice Center Alliance, a program of Alliance for HOPE International, focuses on developing and supporting multi-agency collaboratives and multi-disciplinary models where victims of domestic violence, sexual assault, elder abuse, human trafficking, and other forms of violence can come together in one place.

Contact Information:
(888) 511-3522
https://www.familyjusticecenter.org/

The Spring of Tampa Bay

The Spring's mission is to prevent domestic violence, protect victims, and promote change in lives, families, and communities. Since 1977, they have provided a safe haven and comprehensive supportive services to more than 60,000 abused adults and their children, and have answered calls at all hours of the day and night from well over 150,000 women in crisis.

Contact Information: 24-Hour Crises Hotline: (813) 247-7233

Reach Out/Speak Out

The organization's mission is to help women in need of assistance due to domestic violence; to provide shelter, food, clothing, and the necessities of life; to provide information through books and counseling; to enlist the help of other professionals with domestic violence experience; to speak at faith-based organizations and other community meetings regarding the warning signs of domestic violence.

Contact Information: https://reachoutspeakout.org/

New Millennium Community Church

New Millennium Community Church is built around the five purposes of the church according to Scripture: Evangelism, Worship, Fellowship, Ministry, and Discipleship. The church and Its pastor, Reverend Michael Neely, has a heart for those suffering from domestic violence, welcoming them into the fold and assisting in their healing and restoration.

Contact Information:
8900 N. Armenia Ave., Suite 108
Tampa, FL 33604
(813) 450-2798
http://www.nmcctampa.org/

Other Resources

Florida Domestic Violence Toll-Free Hotline – 1-800-500-1119
National Domestic Violence Toll-Free Hotline – 1-800-799-7233

ABOUT THE AUTHOR

Reverend Michael Neely lives in beautiful and sunny Tampa, Florida, where he is the Senior Pastor of New Millennium Community Church. He received his call to ministry in August of 1986 when he resided in Chicago, Illinois. Since then, he has worked in the capacity of Youth Pastor, Sunday School Superintendent, Director of Evangelism, Assistant Pastor, Church Planter, and now Senior Pastor.

He served as the Assistant Pastor of First Baptist Church of College Hill from September of 2000 until March of 2004 under the leadership of Reverend Abraham Brown. He has a tremendous passion for God's Word; a compassion for all community members; a love for God's people; and a deep commitment to the community. His concern for victims of domestic violence led him to become an executive board member of the Family Justice Center, where he served as a volunteer chaplain and spiritual counselor.

Reverend Michael Neely now serves as a spiritual counselor through the Spring of Tampa Bay and is certified to train clergy in the nuts and bolts of domestic violence. He is also the 2009 recipient of the Domestic Violence Volunteer Award from the Hillsborough County Domestic Violence Task Force.

Reverend Michael Neely is married to Katonya Neely and is the father of one daughter and grandfather of two boys and one girl. He plans to pursue a master's degree in Creative Writing. When Reverend Neely is not working, he likes to bowl, play basketball, and indulge in his second love, which is singing. He is an accomplished Classical Lyric first tenor and loves singing classical music, love ballads, and gospel music.

Made in the USA
Middletown, DE
15 April 2024

52960430R00028